The Wonder of Christmas
Once You Believe, Anything Is Possible
Devotions for the Season

The Wonder of Christmas
Once You Believe, Anything Is Possible

The Wonder of Christmas
978-1-5018-2322-0 *Book*
978-1-5018-2323-7 *eBook*
978-1-5018-2324-4 *Large Print*

The Wonder of Christmas: Leader Guide
978-1-5018-2325-1 *Book*
978-1-5018-2326-8 *eBook*

The Wonder of Christmas: DVD
978-1-5018-2329-9

The Wonder of Christmas:
Devotions for the Season
978-1-5018-2327-5 *Book*
978-1-5018-2328-2 *eBook*

The Wonder of Christmas:
Children's Leader Guide
978-1-5018-2336-7

The Wonder of Christmas:
Youth Study Book
978-1-5018-2334-3 *Book*
978-1-5018-2335-0 *eBook*

The Wonder of Christmas: Worship Planning
978-1-5018-2337-4 *Flash Drive*
978-1-5018-2338-1 *Download*

Ed Robb & Rob Renfroe

THE
# Wonder
OF CHRISTMAS

ONCE YOU BELIEVE,
ANYTHING IS POSSIBLE

Devotions for the Season
by Lori Jones

Abingdon Press / Nashville

**The Wonder of Christmas**
**Once You Believe, Anything Is Possible**
**Devotions for the Season**

# CONTENTS

## Week 3: The Wonder of a Manger

## Week 4: The Wonder of a Promise

## Notes

# Introduction

Christmas is the story of a star shining brightly, a name declared joyfully, a manger waiting expectantly, and a promise given freely. Yes, it is the story of what happened on a bright, starlit night some two thousand years ago in the village of Bethlehem, but it is also the story of what is happening right now, right where you are. Without Christmas we could never fully know the wonder of God with us.

The season of Advent is a gift that invites us to see the world through the lens of what God has done and will do. It is a time to remember God's faithfulness and celebrate God's promises. It is a time to reflect on Jesus and discover how the events surrounding his birth can reawaken us to the wonder of Christmas.

These four weeks of devotions are divided into the four themes of *The Wonder of Christmas*:

- The Wonder of a Star
- The Wonder of a Name
- The Wonder of a Manger
- The Wonder of a Promise

They are arranged thematically, rather than chronologically according to the Christmas story. You are invited to read one devotion each day during Advent, taking time to meditate, reflect, and pray as you invite the Lord to give you fresh eyes to behold the wonder of Christmas. It is the wonder that the God of the universe created us, desired a relationship with us, and came to earth to be with us. It is the wonder that God was willing to give everything so that we could be rescued, redeemed, and restored—forever. May the gift of this wonder be yours this Christmas—and always.

# Week 1

*The Wonder of a Star*

# 1.

## God Sets the Stage

*In the beginning God created the heavens and*
*the earth. Now the earth was formless*
*and empty, darkness was over the surface of the*
*deep, and the Spirit of God was hovering*
*over the waters.*
*And God said, "Let there be light," and there was light.*
*God saw that the light was good,*
*and he separated the light from the darkness.*

*(Genesis 1:1–4)*

Can you recall a time you witnessed something truly amazing? Maybe you vividly remember what it was like to stand at the edge of a vast canyon for the first time, or how you felt as beads of water showered you from a roaring waterfall. Or perhaps the amazing moment you remember was quieter, subtler—the first time your spouse held your hand, the moment a friend's kindness overwhelmed you, when you heard a beautiful piece of music that touched your heart.

Such moments, both big and small, fill us with wonder and awe at the depth and creativity of the God who so lovingly and intentionally created our world and each of us. When we are able to be fully present during these moments, aware of the vastness of God, we are changed. These experiences ignite something within us that longs for glory, majesty, and beauty. They awaken our desire for God.

The world as we know it began in darkness. But God was there in the dark of the heavens. The Bible says that God was "hovering" over the earth, as though eagerly anticipating what was coming next. Then suddenly there was light, and the world—born in God's imagination—began to take shape. The wonder of creation lit the world—with God's light a vital illumination for all the beauty and mystery yet to come.

It is mind-boggling to think that God created *everything*. Take a few minutes to reread today's passage from Genesis 1, lingering on the image of God creating everything out of nothing, bringing meaning and beauty into our world with one spark of life-giving, illuminating light. And one day light would illumine the night sky over Bethlehem with the hope of redemption and the promise that God would be with us always.

The season of Advent invites us to see the world through the gift of wonder—to look for the beauty in what God has done and believe there is more to this world than what we can see or understand; to be amazed by the most wonderful story ever told, a story that continues through each of our lives. You are invited to enter this season with a spirit of curiosity, asking to be astonished anew with God's gifts and trusting God to fill you with wonder.

## Prayer Focus

How does meditating on the story of creation affect your view of God? What attributes of God come to mind as you read Genesis 1? Offer a prayer to God, acknowledging God's creative power in the world and in your life. Ask God to place the gift of wonder in your heart as you prepare for Advent.

# 2.

## *Give Us Eyes to See*

*After Jesus was born in Bethlehem in Judea, during the time of King Herod, Magi from the east came to Jerusalem and asked, "Where is the one who has been born king of the Jews? We saw his star when it rose and have come to worship him."*

*(Matthew 2:1-2)*

Have you ever heard someone tell a truly amazing story? As everyone listens attentively—waiting on pins and needles to hear the terrifying, thrilling, or unbelievable details—the storyteller often concludes with these words: "You had to see it to believe it!"

Often it is easier for us to imagine and believe in something spectacular or extraordinary than to recognize the hidden miracles all around us. The people of Israel had been waiting for generations to finally have a king who would rise up and lead them. For as long as anyone could remember, they had been waiting for the Messiah, the one who would deliver their people. Surely such a person would be born in a castle or palace and be heralded with great fanfare and recognition. Yet he was born to a poor Jewish couple in a lowly stable.

It was an unlikely beginning for a king; the tiny, helpless baby lying in the manger was easy to overlook. But God doesn't always use the obvious. Scripture says, "God chose the foolish things of the world to shame the wise; God chose the weak things of the world to shame the strong" (1 Corinthians 1:27). A baby of humble birth was quietly welcomed into the world by seemingly ordinary parents, yet this was no ordinary baby. He was the promised Messiah, the king of the Jews. Matthew's Gospel tells us that wise men from the east had the eyes to see the sign—to recognize the wonder of a star. *Do we?*

The gift of wonder is what allows us to see more where other people see less; to be surprised again and again by beauty and mystery; to be thankful for the wonderful gifts we have received. By believing in the miracle of Christmas and God's plan to redeem a dying world, we are able to see how God is also waiting in this season—waiting to show us the amazing riches of God's love. Waiting for us to stop and wonder and ask for eyes to see his goodness and grace.

*Lord, give us eyes to see.*

## Prayer Focus

How is God nudging you to have eyes to see the plans for you? In what ways might God be waiting in order to reveal heavenly things to you during this season?

# 3.

## *The Search for More*

> *The star they had seen when it rose went ahead of them until it stopped over the place where the child was. When they saw the star, they were overjoyed. On coming to the house, they saw the child with his mother Mary, and they bowed down and worshiped him. Then they opened their treasures and presented him with gifts of gold, frankincense and myrrh.*
> *(Matthew 2:9–11)*

Images of the Christmas story are familiar to most of us—rocky hillsides, dusty roads, shepherds, sheep, and crude structures are all things we would expect to find in the rural desert land where Jesus was born. Scripture doesn't tell us anything about the wise men's appearance or how they traveled into town, but it's safe to assume their presence in Bethlehem must have created a scene that was out of the ordinary.

We read yesterday that the wise men had the eyes to recognize the wonder of a star. Matthew 2:1 tells us that they were from the east—perhaps Babylonia, which is now modern-day Iraq. The Greek word *magos*, which is used to describe the wise men in the original text, describes them as scholar-priests.[1] This description no doubt means they were educated men—a select few who were very knowledgeable about religion and culture. Certainly they held positions of power and were greatly respected. Even their ability to embark on such a lengthy journey indicates they were men of wealth who probably traveled with a large entourage.

The wise men had "successful" lives in terms of what the world values. They did not need more money or accolades. So why did they put aside everything to go and follow a star? What compelled them to travel hundreds of miles through barren terrain and unknown dangers to find a promised king? What did they hope to gain? What did they long to find?

At one time or another, all of us sense that we are made for more. We ask questions and go on journeys to find the answers. Often we feel that something is missing—that we need something more in order for our lives to be right. But not all of us recognize what this need for *more* truly is. In fact, many people who yearn for more end up focusing on simply getting more of the same—more wealth, more success, more recognition, more possessions, more pleasure—more of everything that has already left them unsatisfied and unfulfilled.

While it seems elusive, the root of this consuming desire is actually no mystery at all. Through Scripture God has revealed the answer: "I have called you by name; you are

Mine" (Isaiah 43:1 NASB). Our hearts long for more than we can see, for something bigger than ourselves, because we belong to God. God has "set eternity in the human heart" (Ecclesiastes 3:11), and so deep within we long for him— no matter our gender, race, or nationality. The psalmist proclaimed,

> *Deep calls to deep*
> *in the roar of your waterfalls;*
> *all your waves and breakers*
> *have swept over me.*
>
> *By day the LORD directs his love,*
> *at night his song is with me—*
> *a prayer to the God of my life.*
> *(Psalm 42:7-8)*

We cannot know all that motivated the wise men to seek Jesus, but we do know that the same God who prompted their journey calls to us today. The longing within each of us is a yearning for something more than this world can provide; we long for our Savior. As Saint Augustine wrote, "Thou hast made us for thyself, and restless is our heart until it comes to rest in thee."[2]

## Prayer Focus

In what ways have you been searching for *more*? Describe the yearnings you are feeling, and ask God to satisfy those longings today.

# 4.

## Signs from God

*Thomas said to him, "Lord, we don't know where you are going, so how can we know the way?"*

*Jesus answered, "I am the way and the truth and the life. No one comes to the Father except through me. If you really know me, you will know my Father as well. From now on, you do know him and have seen him."...*

*"If you love me, keep my commands. And I will ask the Father, and he will give you another advocate to help you and be with you forever—the Spirit of truth. The world cannot accept him, because it neither sees him nor knows him. But you know him, for he lives with you and will be in you."*

(John 14:5-7, 15-17)

Have you ever wondered what it was about the star that made so many people look up and take notice? When we look into a clear night sky, it's easy to be in awe of a mass of brilliant, twinkling stars set against a vast black backdrop. But what was it about *this* star hovering over Bethlehem—the one that set local leaders on edge and prompted some to come from so far away?

Whether the light of this brilliant star was the result of planets coming into alignment during a cosmic phenomenon (as some have hypothesized) or simply an extraordinarily bright star, it was a sign from God. Though the wise men were not the only ones to see the star—after all, you couldn't miss it—they saw the star for what it was; they realized it would lead them to God.

Life is full of signs. *Your* life is full of signs; and when you have eyes to see, you notice signs that point you to God and a life of fullness in God. What stirs you deeply and awakens your heart to the love and majesty of God? If you are a parent, you may have felt it the first time you looked into the face of your child. Perhaps you were amazed at the possibility that anything so wonderful could exist. As your gaze was transfixed upon your child's face, you knew in that moment that the big questions in life have an answer—that this child must be a sign that there is Someone greater than you who is authoring our stories.

Maybe you are stirred when you gaze upon the beauty of a sunset or stand in awe of the majesty of a mountain. Perhaps music speaks to you, pulling out depths of feeling and questions that you cannot express in words. Maybe tragedy and suffering have left you broken but buoyed by a strength you know is not your own, making you certain that only God can get you through the deep valley of pain.

There are so many things in life that defy explanation or understanding. In *The Wonder of Christmas* we read, "Life is full of signs, and what distinguishes the wise from the foolish is the ability to recognize them for what they are."[3] Thankfully, God doesn't leave us to figure out all these mysteries on our own. As Jesus prepared his disciples for his death on the cross, he assured them that he would not leave them alone but would ask God the Father to send a helper, the Holy Spirit, to live within us. Jesus said:

> *"All this I have spoken while still with you. But the Advocate, the Holy Spirit, whom the Father will send in my name, will teach you all things and will remind you of everything I have said to you. Peace I leave with you; my peace I give you. I do not give to you as the world gives. Do not let your hearts be troubled and do not be afraid"*
> *(John 14:25-27).*

God did not leave us alone to rely on our own wisdom. Instead God sent his Holy Spirit to guide us. In wisdom and love, God has declared: "You will seek me and find me when you seek me with all your heart. I will be found by you" (Jeremiah 29:13-14a). May this promise point you to God today.

## Prayer Focus

Do you sense the Holy Spirit leading you in life? Ask for the gift of wonder this Advent and for eyes to recognize God's ways of reaching out and revealing.

# 5.

## *The Word, for Us*

*In the beginning was the Word, and the Word was
with God, and the Word was God. He was with
God in the beginning. Through him all things were
made; without him nothing was made that has been
made. In him was life, and that life was the light of
all mankind. The light shines in the darkness, and the
darkness has not overcome it.*

*(John 1:1–5)*

Long before the star appeared in the sky above Bethlehem,
God was sending God's people signs to tell them of Jesus' birth.
Since the beginning, when God created Adam and Eve, God
had been speaking to his people, reminding them of who and
*whose* they were. Even when things were bleak and the future
seemed dim, God spoke to God's people again and again,
reminding them of the Savior who was to come:

21

*"But you, Bethlehem Ephrathah,*
*though you are small among the clans of Judah,*
*out of you will come for me*
*one who will be ruler over Israel,*
*whose origins are from of old,*
*from ancient times."*

*(Micah 5:2)*

*Nevertheless, there will be no more gloom for those who*
*were in distress…*
*The people walking in darkness*
*have seen a great light;*
*on those living in the land of deep darkness*
*a light has dawned.*

*(Isaiah 9:1, 2)*

*The Spirit of the Sovereign* Lord *is on me,*
*because the* Lord *has anointed me*
*to proclaim good news to the poor.*
*He has sent me to bind up the brokenhearted,*
*to proclaim freedom for the captives*
*and release from darkness for the prisoners.*

*(Isaiah 61:1)*

*Therefore the Lord himself will give you a sign: The virgin*
*will conceive and give birth to a son, and will call him*
*Immanuel.*

*(Isaiah 7:14)*

Though the Old Testament stories of laws, wars, tragedy, and bondage often seem far from our own reality, God's words to his people long ago are meant for us today as well: "For the Son of Man came to seek and to save the lost" (Luke 19:10).

Just as the light of the star pierced the night sky and led the wise men to Jesus, so the light of Jesus has been guiding us toward truth since the creation of the earth. The specifics of Jesus' birth were planned long before the day Mary felt the first pangs of labor. In the beginning, God's plan was written on the stars and trembled through every breath of creation. It became the song of nature, the breath of all life. It shouted through the words of the ancient prophets, planting hope in the hearts of all who longed for and believed in God. God was coming, and God wanted everyone to know.

Jesus, the Word, became flesh and lived among us, walking beside us and reassuring us that there is a good plan in place, that we are not alone, that the author of heaven and earth claims us as God's own and walks with us every moment of our lives. Immanuel, God with us.

## Prayer Focus

John's Gospel says, "[Jesus] came to that which was his own, but his own did not receive him. Yet to all who did receive him…he gave the right to become children of God" (John 1:11-12). *You* are a child of God. Tell God how you feel knowing the great lengths God went to in order to claim you as God's child.

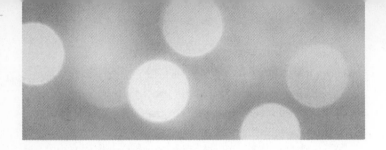

# 6.

## *Courage to Follow*

*The angel went to [Mary] and said, "Greetings, you who are highly favored! The Lord is with you."*

*Mary was greatly troubled at his words and wondered what kind of greeting this might be. But the angel said to her, "Do not be afraid, Mary; you have found favor with God. You will conceive and give birth to a son, and you are to call him Jesus. He will be great and will be called the Son of the Most High. The Lord God will give him the throne of his father David, and he will reign over Jacob's descendants forever; his kingdom will never end."…*

*"The Holy Spirit will come on you, and the power of the Most High will overshadow you. So the holy one to be born will be called the Son of God.… For no word from God will ever fail."*

*"I am the Lord's servant," Mary answered. "May your
word to me be fulfilled."*

*(Luke 1:28-33, 35, 37-38)*

As believers, we should experience Advent as a time of
wonder, surprise, and gratitude—wonder at the great gift that
has been given to us through the birth of Jesus, and surprise
and gratitude at the blessing that God has poured into our
lives by claiming us as God's children.

It's hard to imagine anyone ever being more surprised by
a turn of events than Mary, a young girl whose future was
changed in an instant with the appearance of a mysterious
angelic visitor. It's hard to wrap our minds around the
enormity of what was being asked of Mary—and of Joseph, the
man who had promised to marry her. Scripture does not give
us much insight into the feelings they had about this surprise
announcement, though we know that Joseph's initial plan
was to quietly end the engagement. Perhaps they recalled the
scriptures that had been prophesied from old and were able to
draw some measure of comfort from God's promises. Maybe
they were shocked and afraid, needing to process what was
happening. Perhaps they struggled and questioned and fought
the destiny placed before them.

We don't know what went through Mary's and Joseph's
minds, but we do know that the Lord gave them the courage
they needed to play their parts in a grand plan that would
change the world forever. They chose to follow God and God's
plan, no matter how it would change their lives. Whether in
fear, joy, confusion, or humility, Mary proclaimed,

*"My soul glorifies the Lord*
    *and my spirit rejoices in God my Savior…*
*He has helped his servant Israel,*
    *remembering to be merciful*
*to Abraham and his descendants forever,*
    *just as he promised our ancestors."*
                              *(Luke 1:46-47, 54-55)*

Mary and Joseph followed in obedience, but not everyone in the story had the courage to follow. Herod and others in Jerusalem knew of the prophesied birth of the Messiah, including where he would be born. They were paying attention. They saw the star. But still they did not go looking for him. Why? Could it have been that they were afraid of what they would find? If the Messiah truly had come into the world as had been prophesied, then things would soon change; and perhaps those in power knew that Jesus' birth meant they would have to change too. So when the wise men set out for Bethlehem, Herod and the others stayed in Jerusalem. They did not go on a quest for life-change; they stayed home and continued their everyday lives.

The birth of Jesus demands a response from each of us. Will you stay where you are, like Herod, refusing to relinquish the throne of your own life to a new king? Or, like Mary and Joseph, will you run to your good King, eager to follow the One who was willing to give everything for you?

## Prayer Focus
Is anything keeping you from offering Jesus your whole heart? Talk with him about it.

# 7.

## Bow Down and Worship

*On coming to the house, they saw the child with his mother Mary, and they bowed down and worshiped him. Then they opened their treasures and presented him with gifts of gold, frankincense and myrrh.*

*(Matthew 2:11)*

The wise men made a long journey to find Jesus, and when they arrived they bowed down and worshiped him. *The first thing they did was to bow down and worship him.* Imagine the unlikely, meager surroundings: Jesus' tiny form; no ceremony or fanfare; no guards, no royal advisors, no caregivers other than his parents; a helpless child who had spoken no words and performed no miracles. Yet the Lord moved in their hearts and gave them eyes to see that this baby was the Light of the world, the Savior of mankind. They worshiped him not for what he could do but for who he was.

So much of life is veiled in mystery. There is much we do not understand, yet continually we strive for meaning, understanding, and knowledge. We cannot know the mind of

God or hope to understand everything God does. But when we ask for eyes to see, God will show us evidence everywhere. We will see God in the most unlikely people and places.

When we open our eyes and hearts to God and trust God's goodness, we also can see the evidence of God working in us and through *us*. As Scripture says, "It is God who works in you to will and to act in order to fulfill his good purpose" (Philippians 2:13). As we see God's goodness and strive to know God more, do God's will, and follow the plans God has for us, we can say, like Mary, "I am the Lord's servant. Let it be with me just as you have said" (Luke 1:38 CEB). We can humble our hearts and bow before Jesus in awe of who he is—"the alpha and the omega, the first and the last, the beginning and the end" (Revelation 22:13 CEB).

God sent God's only Son to earth so that we can know God and be in relationship with God. God is leading us daily in ways we do not recognize or understand. God wants to be found by us—whether for the first time or in a deeper way. God never gives up on us, and God will never leave us (Deuteronomy 31:6). Do you know this God who moved heaven and earth to be with you? Do you feel God's presence in your life? Hear God's words today and run to God, bowing down in worship: "I have loved you with an everlasting love; I have drawn you with unfailing kindness" (Jeremiah 31:3).

## Prayer Focus

What signs are pointing you to God this Advent? In what areas of your life do you need to acknowledge God's lordship and leading? Where are you holding back in pride, convinced that you have a better plan? What would it mean for you to bow and worship God?

Week 2

*The Wonder of a Name*

# 1.

## A Different Point of View

*There are different spiritual gifts but the same Spirit;
and there are different ministries and the same Lord;
and there are different activities but the same God
who produces all of them in everyone.*

*(1 Corinthians 12: 4-6 CEB)*

Isn't it interesting that members of the same family oftentimes are wildly different from one another? One sibling is reserved, another is outspoken, and yet another is undoubtedly the peacemaker. Two boisterous parents have a quiet child who prefers to be alone. One sister is extremely frugal, while the other loves a good shopping spree. But all are family, and all share an unbreakable lineage.

The Gospel writers of the New Testament are a bit like a family of brothers, each with his own approach to life, so to speak. The Gospels of Mark and John, for example, do not say one word about the birth of Jesus. Instead, Mark focuses on Jesus' ministry and John on his theology. Both Matthew and Luke tell the story of the Nativity, but each tells it his own way. Matthew's account is more precise and factual, detailing Jesus' royal Jewish heritage and the events surrounding his birth, while Luke's retelling is more like a story, emphasizing how Jesus came as Savior to both Jews and Gentiles. The differences in their deliveries make sense when you consider that Matthew was part of the Jewish establishment and Luke was a Gentile doctor—and therefore an outsider to the Jews.

Though they were very different men with very different perspectives, Matthew's and Luke's accounts of the Christmas story have the same goals in mind—to tell the world of God's master plan to bring the Savior into the world, and to share the extraordinary circumstances surrounding Jesus' birth.

Each of us brings our own unique perspective to the story of Jesus' birth—as well as the story of Jesus in our own lives. Either through birth, choice, or circumstance, we come to Jesus with different points of view that affect our stories: Parent. Child. Insider. Outcast. Damaged. Proud. Rich. Poor.

Though our point of view affects the way in which we come to Jesus, it does not affect the outcome. Jesus says,

*"My sheep listen to my voice. I know them and they follow me. I give them eternal life. They will never die,*

*and no one will snatch them from my hand. My Father, who has given them to me, is greater than all, and no one is able to snatch them from my Father's hand. I and the Father are one"*

*(John 10:27-30 CEB).*

Like Matthew and Luke, our stories are different, but they all point to the same Jesus who came to save us from ourselves. May you boldly use your story to point to him, proclaiming his love and faithfulness over every aspect of your life; and may all who witness your story see Jesus!

## Prayer Focus

What is your point of view regarding Jesus—your view of him? How have you allowed that point of view to unite you with other believers, or separate you from them? What does Jesus want to do with your point of view?

# 2.

# The Many Names of Jesus

*In his days Judah will be saved*
*and Israel will live in safety.*
*This is the name by which he will be called:*
*The LORD Our Righteous Savior.*

*(Jeremiah 23:6)*

Long before his birth, people were talking about Jesus. Prophets predicted his coming. Pharisees fretted over what he would look and act like. The Jewish people prayed for him to deliver them. Creation groaned, awaiting the reconciliation he would bring. Throughout the Bible, we are told what Jesus' coming would mean to the world. Passages about him fill the Old and the New Testaments, giving us numerous and detailed descriptions of how God intended to use his life to save ours. What can we learn from the name *Jesus* that can help to awaken us to the wonder of Christmas?

Take some time to read and meditate on the following Scriptures, paying attention to the different titles used for Jesus (indicated by bold type).

*In his days Judah will be saved*
*and Israel will live in safety.*
*This is the name by which he will be called:*
   ***The Lord Our Righteous Savior.***

(Jeremiah 23:6)

*"For my eyes have seen your* **salvation**,
   *which you have prepared in the sight of all nations:*
**a light** *for revelation to the Gentiles,*
   *and the glory of your people Israel."*

(Luke 2:30-32)

**The Word** *became flesh and made his dwelling among us. We have seen his glory, the glory of the one and only Son, who came from the Father, full of grace and truth.*

(John 1:14)

*[Jesus said,] "I am* ***the good shepherd****. The good shepherd lays down his life for the sheep."*

(John 10:11)

*God exalted him to his own right hand as* **Prince** *and* **Savior** *that he might bring Israel to repentance and forgive their sins.*

(Acts 5:31)

*God put everything under Christ's feet and made him* **head of everything in the church**, *which is his body. His body, the church, is the fullness of Christ, who fills everything in every way.*

*(Ephesians 1:22-23 CEB)*

*Fixing our eyes on Jesus,* **the pioneer and perfecter of faith**. *For the joy set before him he endured the cross, scorning its shame, and sat down at the right hand of the throne of God.*

*(Hebrews 12:2)*

*For there is one God and one* **mediator** *between God and mankind, the man Christ Jesus.*

*(1 Timothy 2:5)*

*I am the* **Alpha** *and the* **Omega**, *the* **First** *and the* **Last**, *the* **Beginning** *and the* **End**.

*(Revelation 22:13)*

Scripture calls Jesus Light, the Word, Prince. Savior, Head of the church, Pioneer and Perfecter of faith, Mediator, First, and Last. Those who were with him called him Teacher, Healer, Prophet, King of the Jews, Messiah. What do you call him?

## Prayer Focus

What name of Jesus resonates most with you? How might meditating on and claiming one of these names bring you closer to Jesus this Advent?

# 3.

## Scriptures and Signs

*Therefore the Lord Himself will give you a sign:*
*Behold, a virgin will be with child and bear a son, and*
*she will call His name Immanuel.*

*(Isaiah 7:14 NASB)*

Do you believe in signs? When your path is unclear and you just can't see a way through, where do you turn for direction, advice, counsel, and comfort?

During the time of the prophet Isaiah, God's people were experiencing war and unrest. The Lord sent Isaiah to speak truth to his people, telling them that although harder times were ahead, God had not forgotten them and one day would send One who would make all things right again. That prophetic promise would be fulfilled through an unsuspecting couple:

*This is how the birth of Jesus Christ took place. When*
*Mary his mother was engaged to Joseph, before they were*

*married, she became pregnant by the Holy Spirit. Joseph her husband was a righteous man. Because he didn't want to humiliate her, he decided to call off their engagement quietly. As he was thinking about this, an angel from the Lord appeared to him in a dream and said, "Joseph son of David, don't be afraid to take Mary as your wife, because the child she carries was conceived by the Holy Spirit. She will give birth to a son, and you will call him Jesus, because he will save his people from their sins." Now all of this took place so that what the Lord had spoken through the prophet would be fulfilled:*

Look! A virgin will become pregnant and give birth to a son,

And they will call him, *Emmanuel.*

(Emmanuel *means "God with us.")*

*When Joseph woke up, he did just as an angel from God commanded and took Mary as his wife.*

*(Matthew 1:18-24 CEB)*

The angel who appeared to Joseph spoke the words that the prophet Isaiah had written long ago: "Therefore the Lord Himself will give you a sign: Behold, a virgin will be with child and bear a son, and she will call His name Immanuel" (Isaiah 7:14 NASB).

Were Mary and Joseph familiar with Isaiah's prophecy? Had they heard those words their whole lives? Were they elated or terrified to play a part in this promise coming true?

Was the mention of Immanuel, God with us, enough to quiet their doubts and assure them that what was happening was from God? Were they comforted by the words of the ancient prophecy during what had to be a mysterious and stressful time in their lives?

Though we have not received angelic proclamations as Mary and Joseph did, we, too, have access to the promises of God in the Word; and we are blessed to know that God's ultimate promise has been fulfilled in Jesus—Immanuel, God with us. We also have the Holy Spirit—the perfect Counselor and Coach—to guide and comfort us through whatever life may bring our way.

With the Word of God at our fingertips and the Holy Spirit living within us, speaking words of life to our hearts and minds, we do not need to search for visible signs in order to follow God—although signs of God's presence and activity are all around us. What a gift it is to know that we have everything we need to hear and follow God!

## Prayer Focus

Ask the Lord to clear your mind of distractions and obstacles so that you can hear God's voice. Thank God for the gifts of the Word and the Holy Spirit, which guide and comfort you.

# 4.

# Jesus, "the Lord Is Salvation"

*Praise be to the God and Father of our Lord Jesus
Christ! In his great mercy he has given us new birth
into a living hope through the resurrection of Jesus
Christ from the dead.*

*(1 Peter 1:3)*

Throughout the Bible we see that names hold great
meaning and often are used to describe significant change.
This is certainly true in the Christmas story.

In *The Wonder of Christmas,* the writers point out a
fascinating connection between Jesus' name and that of
Joshua, one of the Old Testament heroes.[4] We learn of Joshua's
story in the Book of Numbers, in which we find the Israelites
living in the desert. After being freed from Egypt's tyrannical
slavery, they lived for a time in the wilderness; and now they

have made it to the edge of the promised land of Canaan. In Numbers 13, God tells Moses, their leader, to send scouts into Canaan to check out the scene and observe the people who are living there. Moses is instructed to choose twelve scouts, one from each of the original tribes of Judah.

One of the men has the Hebrew name Hoshea, meaning "salvation." We read in Numbers 13:16 that, before sending the spies to explore the land, Moses changed Hoshea's name to Joshua. In doing so, Moses wove together two names—Jehovah (Yahweh), the proper name of the God of Israel,[5] and Hoshea, which means "salvation."[6] This formed a new name, Joshua (*Yehoshua* in Hebrew), meaning "the Lord is salvation,"[7] or God saves.

Why change his name from "salvation" to "the Lord is salvation"? The distinction is not immediately clear until we read about how the scouting trip turned out. Ten of the scouts came back and reported there was no way the Israelites could defeat the Canaanites living there and claim their God-given land. It was too big of a task, they said. But two of the scouts, Caleb and Joshua, had a different take: "The land we crossed through to explore is an exceptionally good land. If the LORD is pleased with us, he'll bring us into this land and give it to us. It's a land that's full of milk and honey. Only don't rebel against the LORD and don't be afraid of the people of the land. They are our prey. Their defense has deserted them, but the Lord is with us. So don't be afraid of them" (Numbers 14:7-9 CEB).

Caleb and Joshua saw the same obstacles as the other scouts. They were not blind or living in denial; they simply believed their God was powerful enough to do what God had promised. They could not achieve victory own their own (*Hoshea,* salvation), but God could do it (*Joshua,* the Lord is salvation). After the Israelites wandered in the wilderness for forty years (the consequence for their disobedience and lack of faith), the Lord did just that. God opened the doors to the Promised Land, and Joshua became the leader who led God's people in.

When the angel announced that Mary and Joseph were to name the child Jesus, that name would have meant something significant to them because *Jesus* is the Greek form of the Hebrew name *Joshua*[8]—"You shall call His name Jesus, for He will save His people from their sins" (Matthew 1:21 NASB). Just as Joshua led God's people out of the desert into the Promised Land, Jesus came to lead us out of the wilderness of sin into the Promised Land of God's eternal presence. Jesus means "the Lord is salvation," pointing us to the eternal power and presence of God.

When he and his people were enslaved in Egypt, Hoshea's name ("salvation") was spoken as a hope, a pipe dream that one day might come true. But through God's power, Joshua's name ("the Lord is salvation") was hope fulfilled. Jesus came, bringing freedom and salvation. Through Jesus, the hope of salvation has become a reality. Amen!

## Prayer Focus

What does your heart hope for today? Can it be that Jesus has already fulfilled that hope and you simply need to claim it? Give thanks today for the fulfillment of all your hopes in Christ.

# 5.

## *The Name that Saves*

*"For God so loved the world, that He gave His only begotten Son, that whoever believes in Him shall not perish, but have eternal life. For God did not send the Son into the world to judge the world, but that the world might be saved through Him."*

*(John 3:16-17 NASB)*

Often it feels as though the state of the world is beyond repair. A quick scan of the headlines can elicit feelings of anger, frustration, disbelief, fear, and even despair. *One step forward, two steps back* seems to be the endless story of humanity.

Have you ever stopped to think how God could send one perfect Son into such a world—as a helpless baby, no less? Jesus had no army, no guards, no protection. He was exposed to the worst that humanity had to offer. Why would God do that? Because there was a big problem in the world—one that was and is at the root of all the injustice, ignorance, violence, and poverty that is so pervasive on this earth. What was the problem? Sin.

In the simplest terms, *sin* is rejection of God. And since the moment Adam and Eve first disobeyed God, sin has stained the fabric of humanity, causing us to look for comfort, purpose, and sustenance outside of God. We might not use the word *sin* often when referring to our daily struggles, but if we take the time to look beyond our temptations or tendencies or basic nature, what we find is sin—an ancient affliction that entangles all of us. Scripture says, "For all have sinned and fall short of the glory of God" (Romans 3:23). *All have sinned.*

God knew that because of the enormity and pervasiveness of the problem of sin, we needed more than just a teacher, counselor, or prophet. We needed a Savior, someone who could bridge the gap and cover our sin so that we can live in fellowship with God. So God sent Jesus.

As we've seen, the angel said to Joseph, "You shall call His name Jesus, for He will save His people from their sins" (Matthew 1:21 NASB). Likewise, "An angel of the Lord appeared to [the shepherds], and the glory of the Lord shone around them, and they were terrified. But the angel said to them, 'Do not be afraid. I bring you good news that will cause great joy for all the people. Today in the town of David a Savior has been born to you; he is the Messiah, the Lord'" (Luke 2:9-11).

The name *Jesus,* which we've seen means "the Lord is salvation,"[9] actively declares that the Lord is the only solution for our sin problem. In his perfect plan, God sent Jesus to earth so that Jesus' life and death could provide the way for us to receive that salvation. Now sin and death no longer hold power over God's children. Jesus is our Lord, the only One who has the power to save. And one day the heartaches and woes of this world will be redeemed and overshadowed by his perfect and loving presence:

> *Then I saw "a new heaven and a new earth," for the first heaven and the first earth had passed away, and there was no longer any sea. I saw the Holy City, the new Jerusalem, coming down out of heaven from God, prepared as a bride beautifully dressed for her husband. And I heard a loud voice from the throne saying, "Look! God's dwelling place is now among the people, and he will dwell with them. They will be his people, and God himself will be with them and be their God. 'He will wipe every tear from their eyes. There will be no more death' or mourning or crying or pain, for the old order of things has passed away."*
>
> *He who was seated on the throne said, "I am making everything new!"*
>
> (Revelation 21:1-5a)

## Prayer Focus

What does the name of Jesus mean to you? How can you put your hope in him today—and every day?

# 6.

## *Children of God*

*Scripture reassures us, "No one who trusts God like this—heart and soul—will ever regret it." It's exactly the same no matter what a person's religious background may be: the same God for all of us, acting the same incredibly generous way to everyone who calls out for help. "Everyone who calls, 'Help, God!' gets help."*

*(Romans 10:11-13* The Message*)*

When the angel appeared to Joseph and revealed God's plan for Jesus' birth, the angel told Joseph to name the baby Jesus "because he will save his people from their sins" (Matthew 1:21 CEB). Today many people debate who "his people" are, but the Bible makes it clear: "If you declare with your mouth, 'Jesus is Lord,' and believe in your heart that God raised him from the dead, you will be saved" (Romans 10:9).

If you believe that Jesus is who he said he was—that he came to earth to die for our sins and was resurrected in order to defeat sin and death—then you are "his people." If you accept God's gift of love and salvation, then God wholeheartedly and joyfully gives you a new name: *Mine*.

Scripture proclaims:

*The one who is the true light, who gives light to everyone, was coming into the world.*

*He came into the very world he created, but the world didn't recognize him. He came to his own people, and even they rejected him. But to all who believed him and accepted him, he gave the right to become children of God. They are reborn—not with a physical birth resulting from human passion or plan, but a birth that comes from God.*

(John 1:9-13 NLT)

*Therefore, there is now no condemnation for those who are in Christ Jesus, because through Christ Jesus the law of the Spirit who gives life has set you free from the law of sin and death.*

(Romans 8:1-2)

*I have called you by name; you are mine.*

(Isaiah 43:1c CEB)

No longer do we have to answer to the old names that sin holds over us: Failure. Unwanted. Forgotten. Sinner. No! In Jesus we are given new names—names that are spoken tenderly over us by our Father:

*I will be a father to you, and you will be my sons and
daughters, says the Lord Almighty.*

*(2 Corinthians 6:18 CEB)*

*I no longer call you servants, because a servant does not
know his master's business. Instead, I have called you
friends, for everything that I learned from my Father I
have made known to you.*

*(John 15:15)*

*For we are God's masterpiece. He has created us anew in
Christ Jesus, so we can do the good things he planned for
us long ago.*

*(Ephesians 2:10 NLT)*

*See how very much our Father loves us, for he calls us his
children, and that is what we are!*

*(1 John 3:1a NLT)*

Son. Daughter. Friend. Masterpiece. Child. Let us "thank
God for this gift too wonderful for words!" (2 Corinthians
9:15 NLT).

## Prayer Focus

Is there anything holding you back from allowing God to call
you *Child*? Will you accept God's claim on you today?

# 7.

## A New Name

*When Jesus came to the region of Caesarea Philippi,
he asked his disciples, "Who do people say the Son of
Man is?"*

*They replied, "Some say John the Baptist; others say
Elijah; and still others, Jeremiah or one of the prophets."*

*"But what about you?" he asked. "Who do you say I am?"*

*Simon Peter answered, "You are the Messiah, the Son of
the living God."*

*Jesus replied, "Blessed are you, Simon son of Jonah, for
this was not revealed to you by flesh and blood, but by
my Father in heaven. And I tell you that you are Peter,
and on this rock I will build my church, and the gates of
Hades will not overcome it."*

*(Matthew 16:13-18)*

The moment we first hear God call our name, speaking "Son" or "Daughter" over us, is a life-changing, life-giving moment. It changes who we are, and we are never the same again.

Throughout the Bible, we read of God changing people's names to signify a new meaning or purpose for them. In Genesis we read that God changed the name of Abram, which means "exalted father,"[10] to Abraham, which means "father of a multitude,"[11] as a sign of God's promise that Abraham would become the father of many nations (Genesis 17:5). Likewise, in the New Testament, we read of Jesus changing Simon's name to Peter, the Greek word for *rock*,[12] so that Peter would forever be reminded of the purpose Jesus had for him: "Now I say to you that you are Peter (which means 'rock'), and upon this rock I will build my church, and all the powers of hell will not conquer it" (Matthew 16:18 NLT).

How did their new names change Abraham and Peter? What must it have been like to receive such a personal and prophetic word from the Lord? Abraham was ninety-nine years old and had no children at the time God changed his name to "father of many nations," so the promise likely seemed impossible. Abraham knew that he had no power on his own to fulfill the promise, but he believed what God had told him; and in time God fulfilled that promise with a son, Isaac—and many generations to follow. And what about Peter? The road he walked as a disciple of Jesus was certainly bumpy, and there were times he doubted his own faith and purpose; but he continued to spread the good news and build Christ's church.

Though both Abraham and Peter sometimes faltered and doubted God's promises to them, they always could remember the names God had given them and be reassured of God's power and presence in their lives.

God's promises are not empty. If God promises something, God will be faithful to fulfill it. That's what God did through his Son, Jesus. God promised to come for you, and God did. God has pursued you through the heavens and the earth in order to call you God's child. Will you claim this name that God has given you? Will you hold fast to the promise regardless of your doubts?

As we walk through this season of Advent, may we claim God's promises fulfilled in Jesus and experience the power and presence of his wonderful name—*Immanuel*, God with us.

## Prayer Focus

What name do you hear God speaking over you today? How do the rhythms of this season help to increase your awareness of the lengths God has taken to give you a new name?

# Week 3

## The Wonder of a Manger

# 1.

# An Inconvenient Journey

*Now in those days a decree went out from Caesar Augustus, that a census be taken of all the inhabited earth. This was the first census taken while Quirinius was governor of Syria. And everyone was on his way to register for the census, each to his own city. Joseph also went up from Galilee, from the city of Nazareth, to Judea, to the city of David which is called Bethlehem, because he was of the house and family of David, in order to register along with Mary, who was engaged to him, and was with child. While they were there, the days were completed for her to give birth. And she gave birth to her firstborn son; and she wrapped Him in cloths, and laid Him in a manger, because there was no room for them in the inn.*

*(Luke 2:1-7 NASB)*

When historians look back on our present-day culture and study our behavior and customs, what will they conclude about us? One of the things they likely will notice is that we are a people devoted to convenience. We are constantly coming up with new and improved ways to get the job done faster and more efficiently than before. Technology has exploded this world of convenience, allowing us to do in seconds what once took hours to complete. It's no wonder that most of us hate to be inconvenienced, becoming frustrated when the unexpected disrupts our plans.

As Mary and Joseph waited for Jesus' arrival, they learned that they would have to pack up and make an arduous journey back to Joseph's hometown. How do you think they must have felt? We think waiting in line at the airport is torture; just imagine traveling approximately eighty miles on foot or the back of an animal while pregnant! Perhaps Mary and Joseph were prepared for the trip and braced themselves for the journey. Or maybe it was a surprise summons and they were shocked at the impossible timing of it all. But in the midst of the unlikely and the inconvenient, God had a plan.

Long ago the prophet had said,

> *But you, O Bethlehem of Ephrathah,*
> *who are one of the little clans of Judah,*
> *from you shall come forth for me*
> *one who is to rule in Israel,*
> *whose origin is from of old,*
> *from ancient days.*
>
> *(Micah 5:2 NRSV)*

Mary and Joseph were forced to travel to Bethlehem at a very inconvenient time for them. It surely must have been a difficult and tiresome trip. And when they arrived, things did not get much better. There was nowhere for them to rest their heads, no proper bed in which to place their newborn baby. The circumstances surrounding Jesus' birth were unlikely and unexpected—and inconvenient for his parents. But it was part of God's plan—a plan to come and rescue us all.

When we are faced with inconvenient circumstances or unexpected disruptions in our plans, we can become frustrated and angry. But in those times, we can know that God is present and working. Romans 8:28 tells us, "We know that all things work together for good for those who love God, who are called according to his purpose" (NRSV).

Could it be that God wants to use even the inconvenient, unlikely, and uncomfortable places in our lives to draw us closer to God and God's purposes? Will we allow the unlikely crib of a manger to awaken us to the wonder of Christmas?

## Prayer Focus
What is your typical reaction to distractions or inconveniences in your life? Ask God to help you to turn to God in those moments for guidance and assurance.

# 2.

## *God Came for You*

*He tends his flock like a shepherd:*
*He gathers the lambs in his arms*
*and carries them close to his heart;*
*he gently leads those that have young.*

*(Isaiah 40:11)*

For many of us, setting out a Nativity scene is an integral part of Christmas decorating. As we take the pieces of the manger scene out of the box, we begin to set the stage as we've imagined it: Jesus in the manger, front and center, surrounded by Mary and Joseph; some farm animals and a few shepherds sprinkled around; perhaps an angel and a star hanging above them all.

The beautiful Nativity scenes in our homes and churches are meant to inspire us during the Advent season, but, in fact, there was nothing romantic about Jesus' birth. It was not picturesque or serene. It likely was not a "silent night" after all. Not only was the birth of their child inconvenient for Mary and Joseph, who were far from home and could not find a proper room; it also must have been somewhat traumatic. Young Mary, barely a teenager, faced childbirth without the women of her family by her side. There was no one to say, "You can do this! That is totally normal. You're going to be okay. It will all be over soon." And how did Joseph feel to be the only one at Mary's side? Surely this was not what he had anticipated either. Did they wonder why God had allowed them to face this all alone? Did they doubt God's plan for them?

When we read the Bible, we get the whole picture—we know the ending of the story. We discover that God was putting countless details into place for the greatest rescue mission of all time. We see that God was coming for the world in the way that only God could. But what if in the midst of this world-changing event God was doing something else—something smaller yet not at all insignificant?

At the same time that God was revolutionizing the world, what if God also was working a miracle in the relationship of Mary and Joseph, binding them together as husband and wife? Think about it. Mary and Joseph were given the gift of being the earthly parents of Jesus, God's Son. They are the only two people of all time ever to have this distinction. *The only ones.* When we consider this enormous and precious task, it's easy to imagine that they must have struggled at some point. Who could understand what they were going through and what they were experiencing? Who could advise and counsel them about what was to come? No one. They needed each other.

So there, in the midst of Jesus' miraculous, earth-shattering birth, God was bringing Mary and Joseph together in a powerful way. Imagine the understanding and solidarity they must have shared in that moment as they held the newborn Jesus close.

While giving them the most important job in the world, God also was tenderly caring for their relationship. Picture Mary and Joseph standing over Jesus as he slept in the manger—tired parents taking in every second of the rising and falling of his tiny chest, wondering at his impossibly small fingers and toes, being enchanted by each coo and smile. *Look at what God has done,* they must have thought. *God sent him just for us.*

Yes, God sent Jesus to save the entire world, but God also sent him just for Mary, just for Joseph. God came for all, but God came just for you too.

## Prayer Focus

In Matthew 18:12-14 (NLT), Jesus says, "If a man has a hundred sheep and one of them wanders away, what will he do? Won't he leave the ninety-nine others on the hills and go out to search for the one that is lost? And if he finds it, I tell you the truth, he will rejoice over it more than over the ninety-nine that didn't wander away! In the same way, it is not my heavenly Father's will that even one of these little ones should perish." Consider today that God moved heaven and earth to send Jesus to save the world—and God also did it just for you.

# 3.

# The Humble Manger

*And she gave birth to her firstborn, a son. She*
*wrapped him in cloths and placed him in a manger,*
*because there was no guest room available for them.*

*(Luke 2:7)*

"Away in a Manger" is one of the most popular hymns we
sing at Christmastime. This sweet, tender song is often one of
the first Christmas carols that children learn and are able to
sing:

> Away in a manger, no crib for a bed,
> the little Lord Jesus laid down his sweet head;
> the stars in the bright sky looked down where he lay,
> the little Lord Jesus, asleep on the hay.
> The cattle are lowing, the baby awakes,
> but little Lord Jesus, no crying he makes.
> I love thee, Lord Jesus: look down from the sky
> and stay by my cradle until morning is nigh.[13]

The hymn creates a serene, peaceful picture of baby Jesus sleeping on the hay, laid in a manger because there was no room in the inn. But when we stop to consider these familiar words, we realize that the scene is actually quite odd, isn't it? The Son of God is sleeping in a feeding trough surrounded by animals. It just doesn't add up. This does not seem to be the best place for a newborn baby, let alone *this baby*—the Christ Child, God's own Son, the Savior of the world. Certainly God could have orchestrated more appropriate circumstances. Why didn't Mary give birth in a nice, clean palace or the home of a local dignitary—anywhere to send a message that this child was special, that he deserved recognition and praise?

God could have made Jesus' birth a national event, but that was not God's plan. From the start, God wanted to set the stage for Jesus' reign. In *The Wonder of Christmas* we read, "The manger was a harbinger of Christ's entire ministry. It spoke volumes about the way the Sovereign Ruler of the universe intended to win back lost children—not by overwhelming us with might but winning us with love."[14]

God did not go to such lengths to send a Son to earth so that we would be his loyal subjects, devoted to him because of his great power. God did not move heaven and earth to sit on a throne and cause everyone to jump to attention at the wave of his hand. No, our God wanted more; God wanted relationship—to restore the relationship that once was with God's creation before sin entered the world. So God used a mighty power to send Jesus to defeat sin and death once and for all.

The manger was only the beginning. During Jesus' ministry, he encountered people who desperately wanted him to become their earthly king, and he showed them that he had a different way. We see this illustrated in Jesus' encounter with a vulnerable woman in John 8:

*And Jesus went to the Mount of Olives. Early in the morning he returned to the temple. All the people gathered around him, and he sat down and taught them. The legal experts and Pharisees brought a woman caught in adultery. Placing her in the center of the group, they said to Jesus, "Teacher, this woman was caught in the act of committing adultery. In the Law, Moses commanded us to stone women like this. What do you say?" They said this to test him, because they wanted a reason to bring an accusation against him. Jesus bent down and wrote on the ground with his finger.*

*They continued to question him, so he stood up and replied, "Whoever hasn't sinned should throw the first stone." Bending down again, he wrote on the ground. Those who heard him went away, one by one, beginning with the elders. Finally, only Jesus and the woman were left in the middle of the crowd.*

*Jesus stood up and said to her, "Woman, where are they? Is there no one to condemn you?"*

*She said, "No one, sir."*

*Jesus said, "Neither do I condemn you. Go, and from now on, don't sin anymore."*

*(John 8:1–11 CEB)*

The Pharisees set up this encounter because they wanted Jesus to explode in an expression of righteous power, showing himself strong; but instead Jesus offered the woman compassion and mercy—a far greater strength than they were capable of themselves. Indeed,

*The LORD is gracious and full of compassion,*
*Slow to anger and great in mercy.*
*The LORD is good to all,*
*And His tender mercies are over all His works.*

*(Psalm 145:8-9 NKJV)*

By coming down and resting in a humble manger, God shows how to lead in a different way. God wants to show tenderness to us in the midst of great power and might. Why? Because God loves us so.

## Prayer Focus

How do you respond to the knowledge that God wants to lead you with tenderness and mercy? How is God speaking tenderly to you today?

# 4.

## _The Great Pursuit_

> "Or suppose a woman has ten silver coins and loses
> one. Doesn't she light a lamp, sweep the house and
> search carefully until she finds it? And when she finds
> it, she calls her friends and neighbors together and
> says, 'Rejoice with me; I have found my lost coin.'
> In the same way, I tell you, there is rejoicing in the
> presence of the angels of God over one sinner who
> repents."
>
> *(Luke 15:8-10)*

In P. D. Eastman's classic children's book *Are You My
Mother?* a baby bird hatches from its egg to find it is alone in
the nest. Having fallen from the tree, the little bird goes on a
quest for its mother—only the bird doesn't really know who it
is looking for. The little bird encounters a kitten, a hen, a dog,
a cow, a boat, and a plane, and it asks all of them the same
question: "Are you my mother?" The baby bird is discouraged
but doesn't give up. Finally, with a little help from a bulldozer,

the baby bird finds its way back to the nest, where its mother has returned with juicy worms. All is well as mother and baby bird snuggle together in the nest. The beloved has been found.

Have you ever lost something dear to you—or to someone you love? Maybe you've spent hours on your hands and knees looking for a lost heirloom or a child's favorite toy that disappeared. Chances are you did whatever you could to find the lost object, because when something is precious to you, you're willing to go to great lengths to get it back.

Luke's Gospel says, "For the Son of Man came to seek and to save the lost" (19:10). Throughout the centuries, God said he was coming to rescue God's people, that they had not been forgotten, that God's covenant would be kept with them. So, when the time was right, God sent Jesus, whose birth was part of a mission to save God's people. Through Jesus' teaching, we see that God is a seeker, always in pursuit of God's people.

In Luke 15, Jesus tells three parables (the lost sheep, the lost coin, and the lost son) to describe God's unfailing love for and pursuit of God's lost people:

> *"'Rejoice with me; I have found my lost sheep.' I tell you that in the same way there will be more rejoicing in heaven over one sinner who repents than over ninety-nine righteous persons who do not need to repent."*
>
> *(Luke 15:6b-7)*

> *"'Rejoice with me; I have found my lost coin.' In the same way, I tell you, there is rejoicing in the presence of the angels of God over one sinner who repents."*
>
> *(Luke 15:9b-10)*

*"'But we had to celebrate and be glad, because this brother of yours was dead and is alive again; he was lost and is found.'"*

*(Luke 15:32)*

As Sally Lloyd-Jones describes so beautifully in The Jesus Storybook Bible, "You see, no matter what, in spite of everything, God would love his children—with a Never Stopping, Never Giving Up, Unbreaking, Always and Forever Love."[15] God was intentionally pursuing us, and the manger is a beautiful picture of the lengths God was willing to go in order to reach us, whatever the cost. Jesus came to earth as a helpless, poor baby, and said, "This is My body which is broken for you" (1 Corinthians 11:24b NLV).

Charles Wesley's beautiful words tell us of God's gift to us through Jesus:

> He left His Father's throne above
> (so free, so infinite his grace!),
> emptied himself of all but love,
> and bled for Adam's helpless race.
> 'Tis mercy all, immense and free;
> for, O my God, it found out me![16]

## Prayer Focus

Meditate on the parables in Luke 15, which describe God's relentless pursuit of you and the joy God has in calling you God's own. How do you feel knowing that God went to such great lengths to rescue you and be in relationship with you? Express your heart to God now.

# 5.

## A New Perspective

*Now Moses was tending the flock of Jethro his father-in-law, the priest of Midian, and he led the flock to the far side of the wilderness and came to Horeb, the mountain of God. There the angel of the Lord appeared to him in flames of fire from within a bush. Moses saw that though the bush was on fire it did not burn up. So Moses thought, "I will go over and see this strange sight—why the bush does not burn up."*

*When the LORD saw that he had gone over to look, God called to him from within the bush, "Moses! Moses!"*

*And Moses said, "Here I am."*

*"Do not come any closer," God said. "Take off your sandals, for the place where you are standing is holy ground." Then he said, "I am the God of your father, the God of Abraham, the God of Isaac and the God of Jacob." At this, Moses hid his face, because he was afraid to look at God.*

*The LORD said, "I have indeed seen the misery of my
people in Egypt. I have heard them crying out because
of their slave drivers, and I am concerned about
their suffering. So I have come down to rescue them
from the hand of the Egyptians and to bring them
up out of that land into a good and spacious land, a
land flowing with milk and honey. . . . So now, go. I
am sending you to Pharaoh to bring my people the
Israelites out of Egypt."*

(Exodus 3:1–8, 10)

Have you ever experienced a "burning bush" moment in your life—a time when something abstract became real to you in a life-changing way? When Moses set out to check on the sheep that day, he didn't expect anything unusual to happen, but the day turned out to be anything but ordinary. As he walked out to meet his flock, Moses had no way of knowing that he would encounter the Living God—or that this encounter would change the course not only of his life but also of all the people of Israel. One day life was normal; the next the world as he knew it was turned upside down.

That's exactly what happened on a starlit night in Bethlehem. Jesus Christ, the Son of God, stepped into our world and changed the relationship between God and humanity. In a manner of speaking, we had seen God in black and white, but then Jesus stepped onto the stage in living color. The birth of Jesus flipped the world upside down, forever changing what it meant for God to love and lead God's people. And the change was unexpected, to say the least.

Jesus came quietly—not in power but in weakness; introduced from a manger, not a throne. The event of his birth was unexpected, as was the person of Jesus. We often associate leaders with forceful, charismatic power. We tend to respect leaders because they accomplish, deliver, fight for, and earn. Why, then, didn't God send Jesus in that way, a way that we could easily understand? Why did Jesus come quietly and meekly—though full of power?

God sent Jesus to earth in a way that announced a new way of understanding the kingdom of God. His life, birth, and death challenge our assumptions and our perspective so that we can see as he sees and value what he values. He is a leader like no other, one who says, "Come to me, all you who are weary and burdened, and I will give you rest" (Matthew 11:28); "I have called you friends, for everything that I learned from my Father I have made known to you" (John 15:15b); "I am the good shepherd. The good shepherd lays down his life for the sheep" (John 10:11).

As we look upon the manger this Advent, may we see and experience the love and tenderness of the God we follow. May we love as God loves and value what God values. May we allow God to set fire to our ordinary expectations and give us extraordinary vision to see what God is doing in the world and how we are to participate.

## Prayer Focus

Has God ever revealed himself to you in a way that completely surprised you? Was it a quiet event or did it come into your life with a bang? How did it change you? Talk with God about how he has used that experience in your life.

# 6.

## *How to Be Human*

*Though he was God,*
*he did not think of equality with God*
*as something to cling to.*
*Instead, he gave up his divine privileges;*
*he took the humble position of a servant*
*and was born as a human being.*

*(Philippians 2:6-7b NLT)*

Christmas forces us to consider Jesus' humanity, and one of the reasons he came down from heaven was to show us how to live here on earth. The people who lived during the time of Jesus were just like us in many ways. They struggled with self-protection and greed. They struggled with comparison. Jesus addressed all of these issues in the parable of the good Samaritan.

A religious scholar asked Jesus what he should do to have eternal life, and Jesus responded by asking what the Law said. The scholar replied,

*"'Love the Lord your God with all your heart and with*
*all your soul and with all your strength and with all your*
*mind'; and, 'Love your neighbor as yourself.'"*

*(Luke 10:27)*

Jesus affirmed his answer, but the teacher wanted a loophole; so he asked, "Who is my neighbor?"

Jesus told him a story about a man who was traveling from Jerusalem to Jericho and was attacked by robbers. They beat him, took his clothes, and left him for dead. A priest came along and passed on the other side of the road. Later a Levite came and also passed by. But then a Samaritan happened by, had compassion on him, and stopped to bandage his wounds. The Samaritan took the man to an inn and paid the innkeeper to take care of him, pledging to pay any extra expenses on his return.

Jesus asked, "Who was the man's neighbor?" The scholar replied, "The one who showed compassion." And Jesus said, "Go and do the same." (See Luke 10: 25-37.)The scholar was asking Jesus, "Who is deserving of mercy?" Jesus essentially responded, "Everyone." The scholar wanted to know, "How much must I give?" Jesus' answer? *Everything.*

As we follow the story of Jesus through the Gospels, we see that Jesus modeled a life of servanthood. What does the life of a servant look like? For us it may look like volunteering at a local food bank or cleaning up the coffee area after church. Living a life of servanthood can look different for each of us—all we have to do is be obedient to those things that God puts before us.

Jesus came so that we could live united with God—now and forever. He walked on the earth so that we could watch and learn from him how to truly be free. He knew we had no strength to do it on our own. His own words to his disciples as expressed in The Message Bible sum it up well:

> *"What I'm trying to do here is get you to relax, not be so preoccupied with getting so you can respond to God's giving....*
>
> *"Be generous. Give to the poor. Get yourselves a bank that can't go bankrupt, a bank in heaven far from bankrobbers, safe from embezzlers, a bank you can bank on. It's obvious, isn't it? The place where your treasure is, is the place you will most want to be, and end up being."*
> (Luke 12:29-34 The Message)

## Prayer Focus

How is God calling you to walk and live with others as Jesus did? Where is God calling you to walk differently, following in Jesus' footprints of grace and servanthood?

# 7.

# A Promise Fulfilled

*"When you come looking for me, you'll find me.*

*"Yes, when you get serious about finding me and want it more than anything else, I'll make sure you won't be disappointed." God's Decree.*

*"I'll turn things around for you. I'll bring you back from all the countries into which I drove you"—God's Decree—"bring you home to the place from which I sent you off into exile. You can count on it."*
*(Jeremiah 29:13-14 The Message)*

Have you ever witnessed a young child playing hide and seek with a parent? The game always ends the same way, doesn't it? The child finds the parent. Why? Because the parent hides in order to be found, so that the child will experience the joy of discovery. The parent could remain hidden until the child gives up or gets bored and loses interest, but that's not the parent's desire. Wanting to be with the child, the parent allows the child to find him or her. It's the same with our heavenly Father.

The manger tells us that Jesus came to earth because God wants to be found by us—in fact, he guarantees it: "'I will be found by you,' declares the LORD" (Jeremiah 29:14a). Have you ever felt that God was hiding from you or was difficult to "find"? Do you feel intimated by reading the Bible, afraid that you won't understand what God is saying? Maybe you ignore the questions you have about God, theology, or church because you think you're not knowledgeable enough to have those discussions with others. Perhaps it seems as though God speaks to those who "get it," and you just don't. Maybe you feel that having faith means never having doubts or questions.

God wants to be found. God wants us to come to the manger. God wants us to find him there because God has good things for us:

> "For I know the plans I have for you," declares the LORD, "plans to prosper you and not to harm you, plans to give you hope and a future. Then you will call on me and come and pray to me, and I will listen to you. "You will seek me and find me when you seek me with all your heart. I will be found by you," declares the LORD, "and will bring you back from captivity. I will gather you from all the nations and places where I have banished you,"

*declares the LORD, "and will bring you back to the place*
*from which I carried you into exile."*

*(Jeremiah 29:11-14)*

These words are not founded in empty hope. They are spoken with surety and power—not as someone who hopes they can get the job done, but as someone who has already delivered. These words are spoken as a promise—a promise that was fulfilled in Jesus. Through a baby in a humble manger, God was revealed fully to us. Our hearts—imprisoned by sin and death—cried out to God, and God answered. God sent Jesus to rescue us, free us, gather us together, and bring us home to God.

## Prayer Focus

What does the wonder of the manger mean for you personally? How can you live in the knowledge that Jesus came for you and fulfilled all of God's promises for you?

# Week 4

*The Wonder of a Promise*

# 1.

## God with Us

*"'My dwelling place will be with them; I will be their God, and they will be my people. Then the nations will know that I the LORD make Israel holy, when my sanctuary is among them forever.'"*

(Ezekiel 37:27-28)

When you are facing a difficult situation, receiving a good word from someone who truly understands what you're going through makes all the difference. Sure, it's nice to get encouragement from those who know about, but don't really understand, your situation; but it can be life-changing to hear someone say, "I've been there, and I know what you're going through." To feel truly understood, rather than just acknowledged, changes everything.

The people of Israel knew much about their God. As the writers point out in *The Wonder of Christmas*, the Israelites who lived before Jesus thought of God in three ways[17]—God *above us*, God *against us*, and God *for us*.

First, they clearly understood the idea of God *above us*. They worshiped and acknowledged God as the Creator of everything and the One who led them. As the prophet Isaiah wrote,

> *"For my thoughts are not your thoughts,*
>     *neither are your ways my ways,"*
>        *declares the LORD.*
> *"As the heavens are higher than the earth,*
>     *so are my ways higher than your ways*
>     *and my thoughts than your thoughts."*
>           *(Isaiah 55:8-9)*

Second, as they acknowledged God's power and authority when they sinned, they believed in God *against us*. And third, when they thought they were doing everything just right, therefore deserving God's favor, they were able to believe in God *for us*.

What do you believe and know about God? When you experience difficulties and hardships, what do you think about God then? Maybe you feel that God is watching from above, concerned about what's going on down here (or perhaps not) while letting it play out on its own. (*God above us.*) Or maybe you've wondered if tragedy and grief are part of God's punishment for our sins. (*God against us.*) Maybe when things are going well and prosperity seems like a reward for good behavior, you feel "blessed." (*God for us.*)

It's tempting to try to put God into one of these categories, but God wants us to have another understanding. This is why, on that first Christmas Day, God turned the tables on all of our preconceived notions about who God is and what God can do. God's desire is not to be God *above us* or God *against us* or even God *for us*. God wants to be God *with us*:

> All this took place to fulfill what the Lord had said through the prophet: "The virgin will conceive and give birth to a son, and they will call him Immanuel" (which means "God with us").
>
> (Matthew 1:22-23)

The Israelites had experienced a long history with God, but they did not believe that anyone could attain an intimate relationship with God. They thought that someone needed to intercede for them—a prophet, leader, priest, or king. But God had made a promise to be with God's people always, and God meant to fulfill that promise in a bigger way than they could have imagined—Immanuel, God *with us*.

## Prayer Focus

Have there been times in your life when you felt that God was *above us, against us,* or *for us?* How does God *with us* change everything? As you meditate today on what it means that Jesus is called Immanuel, "God with us," ask how God wants to transform your preconceived notions of who God is and what God can do in your life.

# 2.

## Come, Thou Long-Expected Jesus

*Eight days later the followers were again inside a house. Thomas was with them. The doors were locked. Jesus came and stood among them. He said, "May you have peace!" He said to Thomas, "Put your finger into My hands. Put your hand into My side. Do not doubt, believe!" Thomas said to Him, "My Lord and my God!"*

*(John 20:26-28 NLV)*

The Israelites did many things in order to be right with God. They sacrificed, repented, washed, and purified. But even with all their rituals and ceremonies, they were unable to realize the deepest cry of their hearts—to be in relationship with God. What they really desired was God *with us*.

During Advent one of the hymns we often sing is Charles Wesley's "Come, Thou Long-Expected Jesus." The first stanza of this hymn reflects Israel's anticipation of their promised Savior and their deep desire for his coming:

> Come, thou long expected Jesus,
> born to set thy people free;
> from our fears and sins release us,
> let us find our rest in thee.
> Israel's strength and consolation,
> hope of all the earth thou art;
> dear desire of every nation,
> joy of every longing heart.[18]

God knew the deepest cry of their hearts because it was God's desire too. God wanted to be with them in a way that was better than they ever could have imagined—a way that would assure them of God's deep and abiding love for them— for all of us. This was God's plan all along. So when it was time, the ancient prophecy was fulfilled, and Mary gave birth to Jesus—Immanuel, God *with us*. That first Christmas Day, God chose to be in the flesh to walk among us, touch us, eat with us, and share life with us.

It is such a great and wonderful mystery that God did this for us. God gave us what we never even knew we needed—a Savior who lived in our world and experienced life just as we do. Jesus felt lonely and rejected, isolated by the very people he was coming to save. He loved people that he lost to death's cold grip. He was tempted, both physically and spiritually. He questioned God's will for his life. He felt physical pain and the mortality of his human body. And yet he also laughed and loved and experienced all the beauty of God's world.

Why is it significant that Jesus came and experienced all these things? It means that we are not alone. We are not alone because Jesus went through everything we do so that we can know he loves us that much. He has delivered us from sin and death so that we can transcend this world and live with him forever.

Sometimes it's not easy to believe that the story is true. When hope seems a luxury and fulfillment is nowhere in sight, we doubt. But even in our doubt, Jesus is gentle and gracious, allowing us, like Thomas, to feel his human scars, look into his eyes, and doubt his love no more.

Just as the first stanza of Wesley's hymn is seeped in hope and anticipation, the second stanza answers that cry:

> Born thy people to deliver,
> born a child and yet a King,
> born to reign in us forever,
> now thy gracious kingdom bring.
> By thine own eternal spirit
> rule in all our hearts alone;
> by thine all sufficient merit,
> raise us to thy glorious throne.[19]

Jesus is the fulfillment of our hope. His coming is the certainty that God is *with us* and does not leave us as those without hope (1 Thessalonians 4:13). Amen!

## Prayer Focus

God the Father knew what we needed to be reassured of God's love for us, and God provided a way. What does it mean to you that Jesus was sent to be God *with us*?

# 3.

## *The Promise of Christmas*

*In the sixth month of Elizabeth's pregnancy, God sent the angel Gabriel to Nazareth, a town in Galilee, to a virgin pledged to be married to a man named Joseph, a descendant of David. The virgin's name was Mary. The angel went to her and said, "Greetings, you who are highly favored! The Lord is with you."*

*Mary was greatly troubled at his words and wondered what kind of greeting this might be. But the angel said to her, "Do not be afraid, Mary; you have found favor with God. You will conceive and give birth to a son, and you are to call him Jesus. He will be great and will be called the Son of the Most High. The Lord God will give him the throne of his father David, and he will reign over Jacob's descendants forever; his kingdom will never end."*

*"How will this be," Mary asked the angel, "since I am a virgin?"*

*The angel answered, "The Holy Spirit will come on you, and the power of the Most High will overshadow you. So the holy one to be born will be called the Son of God. Even Elizabeth your relative is going to have a child in her old age, and she who was said to be unable to conceive is in her sixth month. For no word from God will ever fail."*

*"I am the Lord's servant," Mary answered. "May your word to me be fulfilled." Then the angel left her.*

*(Luke 1:26-38)*

We live by facts. We are trained to operate according to what has already happened, what is certain, what is measureable, and what is definable. For some of us, this makes the concept of living by faith hard to embrace. We desperately want to feel Jesus' presence in our lives. But too often that feels difficult when we can't see him or touch him or hear his audible words. We don't expect a surprise visit from an angel, sharing a word from God. Most of the time we just hope for the best and wonder, *Can God hear me? Is God speaking to me?*

Scripture does not tell us many facts about Mary. We know that she was a cousin of Elizabeth and betrothed to Joseph. But what is important to know is that God entrusted this seemingly ordinary girl with an extraordinary promise—a promise that would change not only her life but also the whole world.

According to Scripture, Mary immediately responded by saying that she believed what the angel said was true. But how might Mary have felt when the angel left and she was all alone with this news? She likely did not *feel* pregnant in that moment. She had been given a promise, but she had to wait for God's timing to experience the fulfillment of it.

As believers, we hold on to the wonderful promise of Christmas: "For God so loved the world that he gave his one and only Son, that whoever believes in him shall not perish but have eternal life" (John 3:16). Through his life, birth, death, and resurrection, Jesus fulfilled that promise, and he gave us another promise—that he is coming back for his children:

> *"Do not let your hearts be troubled. You believe in God; believe also in me. My Father's house has many rooms; if that were not so, would I have told you that I am going there to prepare a place for you? And if I go and prepare a place for you, I will come back and take you to be with me that you also may be where I am."*
>
> (John 14:1-3)

The angel told Mary, "For no word from God will ever fail" (Luke 1:37). As her belly grew and she felt the Christ child stirring within her, she knew that God's promises were true, that God's word did not fail. The promise had come—for Mary, and for us all.

## Prayer Focus

How does the promise of Christmas—that God is *with us* today, tomorrow, and forever—give you hope and peace for your life right now?

# 4.

## A Promise to Keep

*Therefore, imitate God like dearly loved children. Live your life with love, following the example of Christ, who loved us and gave himself for us. He was a sacrificial offering that smelled sweet to God.*

*(Ephesians 5:1-2 CEB)*

It's virtually impossible to make it through the Christmas season without encountering some adaptation of Charles Dickens's classic novella *A Christmas Carol*. The story centers on an elderly miser named Ebenezer Scrooge who despises, well, most everyone, including the poor and the needy around him. He considers them a drain on society and is totally unwilling to spend any of his hard-earned fortune to help those who are struggling on the fringes of society. Scrooge's hard heart extends even to his own employee, Bob Cratchit, whom he pays little for his long hours of work. Cratchit's family struggles mightily, just under Scrooge's nose, but Scrooge has neither the desire nor the insight to notice.

Christmas tales like *A Christmas Carol* often involve transformation. Just as the character of Scrooge is transformed, we are transformed by the promise of Christmas; and we are called to pass that promise on to others. We are called to extend Jesus' hope to those who are hungry and hurting. As the church, the body of Christ, we are called to go where Jesus went and to care for people the way Jesus did—to truly be *with* them and love them. This isn't an easy task. We are easily spooked. We want clear lines showing right and wrong and how we are to treat people on either side of the line.

But when we take a closer look at how Jesus lived and ministered, we see that those who fell in love with Jesus were those who were already in the wrong. They were the outcasts, the adulterers, the doubters, the desperate. And what they saw in Jesus was redemption—something they knew all too well they could not gain on their own. Jesus did not preach at people on a street corner; he had dinner in their homes. He did not publicly shame them; he welcomed them with open arms. The life of Jesus demands that we live with a new perspective of those who live around us.

For those of us who believe the promise of Christmas, we know that Jesus is Immanuel, God with us. And we continue Jesus' mission on earth when we walk alongside others in truth and love so that they see that Jesus is Immanuel, God with them too.

## Prayer Focus
Ask the Lord to open your eyes today so that you can really see the people placed in your path. How can you celebrate the promise of Christmas by extending Christ's love to others this season?

# 5.

## *Weights and Measures*

*What do workers gain from their toil? I have seen
the burden God has laid on the human race. He has
made everything beautiful in its time. He has also set
eternity in the human heart; yet no one can fathom
what God has done from beginning to end. . . . I know
that everything God does will endure forever; nothing
can be added to it and nothing taken from it.*

*(Ecclesiastes 3:9-11, 14b)*

One of the things many of us enjoy during this season is
watching Christmas movies. Some of the funniest ones are
those that feature full-blown Christmas disasters. You know
the kind—someone wants to have the "perfect Christmas"
and goes to insane lengths to plan every detail and decorate
every inch of the house before the extended family arrive.
Everything is perfect—until the people actually arrive. Cue a
series of disastrous events that threaten to ruin the celebration
and leave the family in emotional shambles. Throw in a burned

Christmas dinner and a destroyed Christmas tree, and there you have one spectacular plotline.

We laugh because these movies are hilarious and outrageous, but also because we see the truth in them. We understand the characters' over-the-top desire to make the Christmas season meaningful because the weight of our own expectations for the season can be heavy, even crushing. Maybe you desperately want to spend meaningful time with family and friends, but your time together is thwarted by a predictable angry outburst. Or maybe, just once, you don't want to feel like the black sheep at the table, but you leave feeling as though the people who are supposed to know you better than anyone do not know you at all. We decorate, shop, plan, cook, clean, and party in a quest for meaning and connection. But too often we end up disappointed despite all our hard work. *What does it matter?* we wonder. We were looking for meaning and affection, but we got futility and isolation.

All of us have our hands full of something as we walk into this season—guilt, desire, loneliness, discontent, sadness, anticipation. Holiday advertising promises us plenty—plenty of fun surrounded by plenty of food and presents and friends; plenty of meaning packed into a picture-perfect display. But in all this plenty, we are left wanting. Why? Because we want something from the season that it cannot give. We want something from our family, friends, bank accounts, and churches that they cannot give—because what our hearts desire is simply more of Jesus.

We want God, plain and simple. Theologian C. S. Lewis wrote, "If I find in myself a desire which no experience in this world can satisfy, the most probable explanation is that I was made for another world."[20] Our hearts, having been made by God, deeply desire to be in relationship with our Creator. We long for God's presence, but often we mistake this longing as a desire for things that we can see and taste and touch. We put our hope in things other than God, which causes us to sin. But the miracle of Christmas is that Jesus comes to be with us, turning our faces away from our empty desires and toward him. He says, "Come to me, all you who are weary and burdened, and I will give you rest" (Matthew 11:28). He tells us it's okay, reminding us, "It is not the healthy who need a doctor, but the sick. I have not come to call the righteous, but sinners" (Mark 2:17). He sees our sin; he knows our weaknesses and shortcomings, but he says, "That's why I came. I came to heal. I am the Good Doctor. Let me take care of you."

That is the real promise of Christmas—"For the Son of Man came to seek and to save the lost" (Luke 19:10). Glory to God in the highest!

## Prayer Focus

Acknowledge that the desire of your heart is to be with God alone. Ask God to give you grace and help you feel God's love so that you can give grace to others this season.

# 6.

# *The Abundance of the Promise*

"The God who made the world and everything in it is the Lord of heaven and earth and does not live in temples built by human hands. And he is not served by human hands, as if he needed anything. Rather, he himself gives everyone life and breath and everything else."

*(Acts 17:24-25)*

As we strive to focus on Jesus during Advent, it's easy to be distracted by the mantra of consumerism: *the more, the better!* In many ways it has become a season of excess, an excuse to go over the top with decorations and food and gifts. You can never have too many lights on the house, parties to attend, or presents under the tree, right? Indulging in the festivities of the season can be harmless enough—after all, it *is* a celebration.

But our culture seems to have adopted the mind-set of more in regards to every aspect of our lives. We are bombarded daily with messages that tell us we need more of this or that in order to live a happy life. Many of us have come to believe the myth of scarcity—the idea that we do not have enough of what we need.

We all buy into the myth of scarcity in different areas of our lives, whether we feel there is never enough time, money, resources, or possessions. And when we buy into this myth, we close our hands tightly around what we already have, falling into greed and self-protection. (Remember Scrooge?)

When these feelings creep in during Advent, we need to turn our eyes to the wonder of Christmas—to the reminder that Jesus came to earth to remind us of his abundant love and resources: "For you know the grace of our Lord Jesus Christ, that though he was rich, yet for your sake he became poor, so that you through his poverty might become rich" (2 Corinthians 8:9). Through Jesus we have access to the limitless abundance of our heavenly Father, who gives us everything we need in order to love and serve others. We do not need to worry about not having enough, for God has given us "everything we need for life and for holy living" (2 Peter 1:3 NLV).

By serving and giving freely to others, we pass on the promise of God's abundant love, remembering what God has done for us. Serving is for our good, not for God's. Acts 17:25 tells us that God is "not served by human hands, as if he needed anything. Rather, he himself gives everyone life and breath and everything else." We serve, not because God *needs* us to serve. As Scripture points out, God is fully able to do any work without help. But when we serve, we are reminded of God's great love and provision for us, which leads us to worship through loving and serving others.

## Prayer Focus

Consider the ways you are living with an attitude of scarcity. Confess this to the Lord and ask to be led in some practical ways so you can "keep" the promise of Christmas this season by showing others the abundant love of God.

# 7.

## *The Promise, for You*

*But when the fullness of the time came, God sent forth
His Son, born of a woman, born under the Law, so
that He might redeem those who were under the Law,
that we might receive the adoption as sons. Because
you are sons, God has sent forth the Spirit of His Son
into our hearts, crying, "Abba! Father!" Therefore you
are no longer a slave, but a son; and if a son, then an
heir through God.*

(Galatians 4:4-7 NASB)

Christmas is the story of a star shining bright, a name
declared in joy, a manger humbly waiting, and a promise
given freely. Yes, it is the story of what happened on a bright,
starlit night some two thousand years ago in the village of
Bethlehem, but it also is the story of what is happening right
now, right where we are. It is a story filled with wonder.

It is a story of wonder that the Author of Creation, who breathed life into beings made in God's image, desires a relationship with us. It is a story of wonder that because our relationship was broken by sin, God came to earth so that the relationship could be restored. It is a story of wonder that God was willing to give everything so that we can be with God now and forever.

Once we believe in the wonder of Christmas, anything is possible! Knowing that we matter to the God who created the universe and who loves each one of us personally reassures us that "with God all things are possible" (Matthew 19:26).

Many years after the angel appeared to the shepherds over Bethlehem, another angel appeared to the Apostle John with a holy vision:

> *Then I saw a new heaven and a new earth, for the former heaven and the former earth had passed away, and the sea was no more. I saw the holy city, New Jerusalem, coming down out of heaven from God, made ready as a bride beautifully dressed for her husband. I heard a loud voice from the throne say, "Look! God's dwelling is here with humankind. He will dwell with them, and they will be his peoples. God himself will be with them as their God. He will wipe away every tear from their eyes. Death will be no more. There will be no mourning, crying, or pain anymore, for the former things have passed away." Then the one seated on the throne said, "Look! I'm making all things new." He also said, "Write this down,*

*for these words are trustworthy and true." Then he said to me, "All is done. I am the Alpha and the Omega, the beginning and the end. To the thirsty I will freely give water from the life-giving spring."*

(Revelation 21:1-6 CEB)

The wonder of Christmas is that God fulfilled his promise to come for God's people, and God continues to pursue us. God is continually working in and through us, transforming us and making us new. A star, a name, a manger, a promise. *Immanuel, God with us.*

## Prayer Focus

Thank the Lord for the promise to be Immanuel, God with us—today, tomorrow, and forever. Ask for a heart that can celebrate and live in the light of this great gift today and every day.

# Notes

1. *The Free Dictionary*, s.v. "Magi," accessed June 3, 2016, http://encyclopedia2 .thefreedictionary.com/Magoi.

2. Saint Augustine of Hippo, *The Confessions of Saint Augustine* (Stillwell, KS: Digireads.com Publishing, 2005), 25.

3. Ed Robb and Rob Renfroe, *The Wonder of Christmas* (Nashville: Abingdon Press, 2016), 25.

4. See Ed Robb and Rob Renfroe, *The Wonder of Christmas*, 50-52.

5. *Strong's Concordance Online*, s.v. "Yhvh" (Jehovah), accessed June 7, 2016, http://biblehub.com/hebrew/3068.htm.

6. *Strong's Concordance Online*, s.v. "Hoshea," accessed June 7, 2016, http://biblehub.com/hebrew/1954.htm.

7. *Strong's Concordance Online*, s.v. "Yehoshua," accessed June 7, 2016, http://biblehub.com/hebrew/3091.htm.

8. *Strong's Concordance Online*, s.v. "Iésous," accessed June 9, 2016, http://biblehub.com/greek/2424.htm.

9. Ibid.

10. *Strong's Concordance Online*, s.v. "Abram," accessed June 9, 2016, http://biblehub.com/hebrew/87.htm.

11. *Strong's Concordance Online*, s.v. "Abraham," accessed June 9, 2016, http://biblehub.com/hebrew/85.htm.

12. *Strong's Concordance Online*, s.v. "Petros," accessed June 9, 2016, http://biblehub.com/greek/4074.htm.

13. "Away in a Manger," *The United Methodist Hymnal* (Nashville: The United Methodist Publishing House, 1989), 217.

14. See Ed Robb and Rob Renfroe, *The Wonder of Christmas*, 74.

15. Sally Lloyd-Jones, *The Jesus Storybook Bible* (Grand Rapids, MI: Zonderkidz, 2007), 36.

16. Charles Wesley, "And Can It Be That I Should Gain," *The United Methodist Hymnal* (Nashville: The United Methodist Publishing House, 1989), 363.

17. See Ed Robb and Rob Renfroe, *The Wonder of Christmas*, 101.

18. Charles Wesley, "Come, Thou Long-Expected Jesus," *The United Methodist Hymnal* (Nashville: The United Methodist Publishing House, 1989), 196.

19. Ibid.

20. C. S. Lewis, *Mere Christianity* (New York: Simon & Schuster, 1996), 121.